Lyla Grace
Has Manners!
DO YOU?

Written by
Julie Perkins

Illustrated by
Tammy Jo Bethune

AuthorHouse™
1663 Liberty Drive
Bloomington, IN 47403
www.authorhouse.com
Phone: 1 (800) 839-8640

Benefits of this book is donated to the "Mighty Acorn Foundation".
Adoption of Children

Published by AuthorHouse: 02/23/2016

ISBN: 978-1-5049-7879-8 (sc)
ISBN: 978-1-5049-7856-9 (hc)
ISBN: 978-1-5049-7880-4 (e)

Library of Congress Control Number: 2016902380

Print information available on the last page.

This book is printed on acid-free paper.

author**HOUSE**®

Acknowledgement

My inspiration for this children's book came from my:

Granddaughter Lyla Grace &

Grandsons Phoenix and Carson.

Thank you to all my family and friends for your love and support.

A special thank you to my good friend

Dawn Chatwood for her support, guidance and

encouraging words.

This book is dedicated to

"Little Miss Special", Lyla Grace.

Lyla Grace is a blue-eyed girl with hair of gold. She loves to smile at everyone and makes them feel good! Her kindness shows through in everything she does.

Lyla Grace shows her good manners by giving flowers to her friends and family to make them feel good.

DO YOU?

Lyla Grace opens up the door for her friends and family. When she is at the store with her mommy, she opens the door for people who need help.

DO YOU?

5

Lyla Grace helps carry shopping bags for her mother when they are shopping.

DO YOU?

Lyla Grace helps feed and water her pets and takes them for their daily walks. Come bath time, she helps her daddy wash them too!

DO YOU?

Lyla Grace makes a funny cat face and it makes people smile and laugh when they see it. Lyla Grace likes making people feel good!

DO YOU?

Lyla Grace helps with the cooking. She loves to help her mother in the kitchen preparing meals, baking and even cleaning up. She is such a good helper for her mother.

ARE YOU?

Lyla Grace helps her daddy pick up wood for the fireplace. She rakes leaves and helps clean up the yard.

DO YOU?

Some polite words Lyla Grace says are:

Excuse Me!

Good Morning!

How are you?

Please!

Thank YOU!

Do YOU say any of these?

Lyla Grace wants you to remember good manners because it shows kindness to all of those around you!

Please and thank you.

I love you.

welcome !

19

 **Julie Perkins** lives in Roanoke, Indiana, near Fort Wayne. She has taught in Illinois, Kentucky, Tennessee and Florida during her teaching career.

Julie has taught over 30 years in Elementary and Secondary Education. She has taught most every grade from K through 12 throughout her career. She has maintained an active role in Education.

She is an author in a collaborative teachers manual for the state of Tennessee as well as in Kentucky.

Julie is a Writing Consultant for grades K-5. She teaches Strategies for Writing Prompt Instruction giving teachers the ability to be on the cutting edge of success in teaching and grading writing prompts.

- Julie has a proven track record of improving student scores on mandated Writing Assessment Tests
- She improves writing throughout all grades and classes
- She allows professionals to use a rubric
- She covers all subjects (including manners)

Contact Julie if you wish for Julie to do a Professional Development Day for your school system or book purchase.

Contact Information: julieperkinsauthor@gmail.com

Julie believes every child should be taught manners. Parents and Teachers should be made aware of how important it is to teach children manners. Manners travel with you all your life and it has been proven that those who have manners have a greater advantage for success.

Having good manners leaves a lasting impression with other people in your life.

Tammy holds Associates Degrees in Psychology and Registered Nurse. She studied Art classes for five years with Ales Pancner. She is an artist and illustrator for greeting cards and paintings. Her whimsical greeting cards are in local boutiques in Roanoke and Fort Wayne, Indiana.

Tammy@hyndmaninc.com

ArtforLifestudio.etsy.com